Kugelhopf CookBook 101

A Culinary Journey Through Irresistible Bundt Cakes

While every precaution has been taken in the preparation of this book, the publisher assumes no responsibility for errors or omissions, or for damages resulting from the use of the information contained herein.

KUGELHOPF COOKBOOK 101

First edition. December 10, 2023.

ISBN: 979-8223979210

Written by Jose Maria.

Table of Contents

Jose Maria

Chapter (1) Origin and History of Kugelhopf:

a. Origin:

The Kugelhopf, also spelled Gugelhupf, has its roots in Central Europe, with a history dating back centuries. The name "Kugelhopf" is derived from the German word "Gugelhupf," and variations of this cake are found in several European countries, each with its own unique twist.

b. Significance in Various Cultures:

Germany and Austria: The Kugelhopf is often associated with German and Austrian baking traditions. It has been a staple in celebrations and festive occasions, gaining popularity not only for its delightful taste but also for its distinctive ring shape.

France: In the Alsace region of France, which shares a cultural history with Germany, the Kugelhopf has become a symbol of French patisserie. It's enjoyed during special occasions and is sometimes referred to as "Kougelhopf."

Switzerland: The Kugelhopf has also found its way into Swiss cuisine, where it is cherished as a sweet treat. Swiss variations may include local ingredients, adding to the diversity of Kugelhopf recipes.

Eastern Europe: Variations of the Kugelhopf are present in Eastern European countries such as Poland and Hungary, where it is enjoyed as part of traditional festivities and family gatherings.

Jewish Cuisine: The Kugelhopf has also made its mark in Jewish cuisine, particularly in Ashkenazi Jewish communities. It is sometimes prepared as a sweet bread and served during holidays and celebrations.

Versatile Adaptations: Over the years, the Kugelhopf has undergone various adaptations, both in sweet and savory forms. Its ability to blend with different flavors and ingredients has contributed to its widespread popularity across diverse culinary traditions.

The Kugelhopf's significance goes beyond its delicious taste; it represents a cultural and historical connection, reflecting the diversity and shared heritage of European culinary traditions. As it continues to be a beloved dessert, its legacy endures in kitchens around the world.

Chapter (2) Essential Tools and Ingredients for Kugelhopf:

a. Specialized Kugelhopf Pan:

The distinctive shape of the Kugelhopf is achieved using a specialized Kugelhopf pan. This pan typically has a fluted, bundt-like design with a central tube. The shape helps the cake cook evenly and ensures an attractive presentation.

b. Key Ingredients and Their Role in the Recipe:

Flour:

All-purpose flour provides the structure for the cake. It contains the necessary gluten to give the Kugelhopf its characteristic texture.

Butter:

Unsalted butter adds moisture and rich flavor to the cake. It also contributes to the tender crumb.

Sugar:

Granulated sugar sweetens the cake and contributes to its texture. It also aids in creating a golden crust during baking.

Eggs:

Eggs act as a binding agent and provide structure to the cake. They also contribute to its moisture and help with leavening.

Liquid (Milk or Yogurt):

Liquid ingredients add moisture and help create the desired consistency. Milk or yogurt is often used in Kugelhopf recipes.

Baking Powder:

Baking powder is a leavening agent that helps the cake rise, creating a light and airy texture.

Flavorings (e.g., Vanilla Extract, Almond Extract):

Flavor extracts enhance the taste of the Kugelhopf. Vanilla and almond extracts are commonly used for their aromatic qualities.

Nuts or Ground Almonds:

Ground almonds or other nuts contribute to the cake's flavor and add a delightful texture.

Salt:

Salt enhances the overall flavor and balances the sweetness of the cake.

c. Substitutions and Variations:

Flour Substitutions:

Experiment with different flours such as whole wheat or almond flour for a unique flavor and texture.

Sweeteners:

Substitute some or all of the granulated sugar with alternatives like honey or maple syrup for a different sweetness profile.

Dairy-Free Options:

Use plant-based alternatives like almond milk or coconut yogurt for a dairy-free version.

Flavor Additions:

Get creative with add-ins like chocolate chips, dried fruits, or citrus zest to customize the flavor.

Savory Variations:

For savory Kugelhopf, consider incorporating herbs, cheese, or ingredients like sun-dried tomatoes for a unique twist.

Gluten-Free Options:

Explore gluten-free flours like rice flour or a gluten-free flour blend for those with dietary restrictions.

Spices:

Experiment with spices such as cinnamon, nutmeg, or cardamom for a spiced variation.

Remember, the Kugelhopf is a versatile canvas, allowing for a wide range of substitutions and variations to suit individual preferences and dietary needs.

Chapter (3) Mastering the Basic Kugelhopf Recipe:

a. Step-by-Step Instructions:

Ingredients:

- 2 1/2 cups all-purpose flour
- 1 cup unsalted butter, softened
- 1 cup granulated sugar
- 4 large eggs
- 1 teaspoon almond extract
- 1 cup milk
- 1 cup ground almonds
- 1 tablespoon baking powder
- 1/2 teaspoon salt
- Powdered sugar for dusting

Instructions:

Preheat and Prepare:

Preheat your oven to 350°F (175°C). Grease and flour your Kugelhopf pan thoroughly to prevent sticking.

Cream Butter and Sugar:

In a large bowl, cream together the softened butter and granulated sugar until light and fluffy.

Add Eggs and Extract:

Add the eggs one at a time, beating well after each addition. Stir in the almond extract for a delightful flavor.

Combine Dry Ingredients:

In a separate bowl, whisk together the all-purpose flour, ground almonds, baking powder, and salt.

Alternate Mixing:

Gradually add the dry ingredients to the wet ingredients, alternating with the milk. Begin and end with the dry ingredients. Mix until just combined.

Pour into Pan:

Pour the batter into the prepared Kugelhopf pan, ensuring an even distribution.

Bake:

Bake in the preheated oven for 50-60 minutes or until a toothpick inserted into the center comes out clean.

Cooling:

Allow the Kugelhopf to cool in the pan for 15 minutes before transferring it to a wire rack to cool completely.

Dust with Powdered Sugar:

Once cooled, dust the Kugelhopf with powdered sugar for a decorative finish.

b. Tips for Achieving the Perfect Texture and Flavor:

Room Temperature Ingredients:

Ensure that ingredients like butter, eggs, and milk are at room temperature. This helps in achieving a smooth batter.

Proper Mixing:

Mix the batter just until the ingredients are combined. Overmixing can result in a dense cake.

Greasing the Pan:

Thoroughly grease and flour the Kugelhopf pan to prevent the cake from sticking.

Even Distribution:

Distribute the batter evenly in the pan to ensure uniform baking.

Check for Doneness:

Use a toothpick to check for doneness. If it comes out clean or with a few moist crumbs, the Kugelhopf is ready.

Flavor Enhancements:

Enhance the flavor by using high-quality extracts and fresh ingredients.

c. Common Mistakes and Troubleshooting:

Dry Cake:

Overbaking or using too much flour can lead to a dry cake. Ensure accurate measurements and monitor baking time.

Sticking to the Pan:

Inadequate greasing of the pan may cause sticking. Grease generously and use a non-stick pan if available.

Collapsed Center:

Overmixing the batter or opening the oven door too early in the baking process can result in a collapsed center. Be gentle when mixing and avoid unnecessary oven opening.

Uneven Baking:

Ensure the oven is properly preheated, and the Kugelhopf pan is placed in the center. Rotate the pan if needed for even baking.

Flat Top:

Use fresh baking powder and ensure it's evenly distributed in the batter. Also, check the expiration date of the baking powder.

Lack of Flavor:

If the flavor is lacking, consider adding a bit more of the flavor extracts or incorporating additional spices or zest.

By following these step-by-step instructions, tips, and troubleshooting advice, you'll be on your way to mastering the art of baking a perfect and delicious Kugelhopf every time.

Chapter (4) Sweet Varieties of Kugelhopf:

a. Classic Almond Kugelhopf:

Ingredients:

- 2 1/2 cups all-purpose flour
- 1 cup unsalted butter, softened
- 1 cup granulated sugar
- 4 large eggs
- 1 teaspoon almond extract
- 1 cup milk
- 1 cup ground almonds
- 1 tablespoon baking powder
- 1/2 teaspoon salt
- Powdered sugar for dusting

Instructions:

Follow the step-by-step instructions provided earlier for the Mastering the Basic Kugelhopf Recipe. Add 1 teaspoon of almond extract to the batter to enhance the almond flavor. Dust the baked Kugelhopf with powdered sugar before serving.

b. Chocolate Swirl Kugelhopf:
Additional Ingredients:

- 1/2 cup cocoa powder
- 1/4 cup sugar
- 1/4 cup melted dark chocolate

Instructions:

1. After mixing the main batter, set aside 1 cup of the batter in a separate bowl.
2. Mix the cocoa powder, sugar, and melted dark chocolate into the reserved batter to create a chocolate mixture.
3. Pour half of the almond batter into the prepared pan.
4. Spoon dollops of the chocolate mixture on top and use a knife to swirl it into the almond batter.
5. Add the remaining almond batter and repeat the swirling process.
6. Bake as directed in the Mastering the Basic Kugelhopf Recipe. Allow to cool and dust with powdered sugar before serving.

c. Lemon-Blueberry Bliss Kugelhopf:
Additional Ingredients:

- Zest of 1 lemon
- 1 cup fresh or frozen blueberries

Instructions:

1. Add the lemon zest to the batter when creaming the butter and sugar.
2. Toss the blueberries in a little flour to coat them (to prevent sinking) before folding them into the batter just before pouring into the pan.
3. Bake as directed in the Mastering the Basic Kugelhopf Recipe. Allow the Kugelhopf to cool before serving.

These sweet variations add delightful twists to the traditional Kugelhopf, offering a range of flavors to suit different preferences. Enjoy the richness of almond, the indulgence of chocolate, or the refreshing combination of lemon and blueberry in these delicious sweet Kugelhopf varieties.

Chapter (5) Savory Twists of Kugelhopf:

a. Herbed Cheese Kugelhopf:
   Additional Ingredients:

- 1 cup grated Gruyère or Swiss cheese
- 1/4 cup chopped fresh herbs (such as parsley, chives, and thyme)

Instructions:

1. Follow the Mastering the Basic Kugelhopf Recipe steps, adding the grated cheese and chopped herbs during the mixing process.
2. Ensure even distribution of cheese and herbs in the batter.
3. Bake as directed in the Mastering the Basic Kugelhopf Recipe. Allow the savory Kugelhopf to cool before slicing and serving.

b. Sundried Tomato and Olive Kugelhopf:
Additional Ingredients:

- 1/2 cup chopped sundried tomatoes (drained if in oil)
- 1/2 cup chopped Kalamata olives

Instructions:

1. Follow the Mastering the Basic Kugelhopf Recipe steps, adding the sundried tomatoes and olives during the mixing process.
2. Ensure even distribution of tomatoes and olives in the batter.
3. Bake as directed in the Mastering the Basic Kugelhopf Recipe. Allow the savory Kugelhopf to cool before slicing and serving.

c. Pesto Parmesan Kugelhopf:
Additional Ingredients:

- 1/4 cup prepared basil pesto
- 1/2 cup grated Parmesan cheese

Instructions:

1. Follow the Mastering the Basic Kugelhopf Recipe steps, adding the pesto and grated Parmesan cheese during the mixing process.
2. Ensure even distribution of pesto and Parmesan in the batter.
3. Bake as directed in the Mastering the Basic Kugelhopf Recipe. Allow the savory Kugelhopf to cool before slicing and serving.

These savory variations of Kugelhopf bring a new dimension to this traditional cake. The combination of herbs, cheeses, and savory ingredients adds a delightful twist that makes these savory Kugelhopf variations perfect for brunch, appetizers, or as a side dish for soups and salads. Enjoy the savory goodness!

Chapter (6) Festive and Seasonal Creations of Kugelhopf:

a. Pumpkin Spice Kugelhopf (Fall):
Additional Ingredients:

- 1 cup canned pumpkin puree
- 1 teaspoon ground cinnamon
- 1/2 teaspoon ground nutmeg
- 1/4 teaspoon ground cloves

Instructions:

1. Follow the Mastering the Basic Kugelhopf Recipe steps, incorporating the pumpkin puree and spices during the mixing process.
2. Ensure even distribution of pumpkin and spices in the batter.
3. Bake as directed in the Mastering the Basic Kugelhopf Recipe. Allow the Pumpkin Spice Kugelhopf to cool before serving.

b. Cranberry Orange Kugelhopf (Winter):
Additional Ingredients:

- 1 cup fresh or frozen cranberries (chopped)
- Zest of 1 orange
- 1/4 cup orange juice

Instructions:

1. Follow the Mastering the Basic Kugelhopf Recipe steps, adding the chopped cranberries and orange zest during the mixing process.
2. Substitute 1/4 cup of the milk with fresh orange juice for added citrus flavor.
3. Bake as directed in the Mastering the Basic Kugelhopf Recipe. Allow the Cranberry Orange Kugelhopf to cool before serving.

c. Fresh Berry Burst Kugelhopf (Summer):

Additional Ingredients:

- 1 cup mixed fresh berries (such as blueberries, raspberries, and strawberries)
- 1 tablespoon lemon zest

Instructions:

1. Follow the Mastering the Basic Kugelhopf Recipe steps, gently folding in the mixed fresh berries and lemon zest just before pouring the batter into the pan.
2. Bake as directed in the Mastering the Basic Kugelhopf Recipe. Allow the Fresh Berry Burst Kugelhopf to cool before serving.

These seasonal variations of Kugelhopf capture the essence of each season with the addition of complementary flavors. Whether it's the warmth of pumpkin and spices in the fall, the tartness of cranberries in winter, or the burst of fresh berries in summer, these festive Kugelhopf creations are perfect for celebrating the flavors of each season. Enjoy the seasonal delights!

Chapter (7) Gluten-Free and Vegan Options of Kugelhopf:

a. Almond Flour Kugelhopf (Gluten-Free):
   Ingredients:

- 2 1/2 cups almond flour
- 1 cup unsalted butter, softened (or vegan butter for a vegan option)
- 1 cup coconut sugar (or your preferred sweetener)
- 4 flax eggs (4 tablespoons ground flaxseeds + 12 tablespoons water)
- 1 teaspoon almond extract
- 1 cup almond milk (or any non-dairy milk)
- 1 tablespoon baking powder
- 1/2 teaspoon salt
- Powdered sugar for dusting

Instructions:

1. Preheat your oven to 350°F (175°C). Grease and flour a gluten-free Kugelhopf pan.
2. In a bowl, prepare the flax eggs by mixing ground flaxseeds with water. Let it sit for a few minutes until it thickens.
3. In a large bowl, cream together the softened butter and coconut sugar.
4. Add the flax eggs and almond extract to the butter mixture. Mix well.
5. In a separate bowl, whisk together almond flour, baking powder, and salt.
6. Gradually add the dry ingredients to the wet ingredients, alternating with almond milk. Begin and end with the dry

ingredients.

7. Pour the batter into the prepared Kugelhopf pan.
8. Bake for 50-60 minutes or until a toothpick inserted into the center comes out clean.
9. Allow the cake to cool in the pan for 15 minutes before transferring it to a wire rack to cool completely.
10. Dust the Almond Flour Kugelhopf with powdered sugar before serving.

b. Vegan Chocolate Banana Kugelhopf:
Ingredients:

- 2 1/2 cups all-purpose flour (or a gluten-free flour blend for a gluten-free version)
- 1 cup mashed ripe bananas (about 3 medium-sized bananas)
- 1 cup coconut sugar (or your preferred sweetener)
- 1/2 cup vegetable oil
- 1/4 cup cocoa powder
- 1 cup almond milk (or any non-dairy milk)
- 1 tablespoon baking powder
- 1/2 teaspoon salt
- 1 teaspoon vanilla extract
- 1/2 cup dairy-free chocolate chips (optional)
- Powdered sugar for dusting

Instructions:

1. Preheat your oven to 350°F (175°C). Grease and flour a Kugelhopf pan.
2. In a large bowl, mix together mashed bananas, coconut sugar, vegetable oil, and almond milk.
3. In a separate bowl, whisk together flour, cocoa powder, baking powder, and salt.
4. Gradually add the dry ingredients to the wet ingredients, mixing until well combined.
5. Stir in the vanilla extract and chocolate chips if using.
6. Pour the batter into the prepared Kugelhopf pan.
7. Bake for 50-60 minutes or until a toothpick inserted into the center comes out clean.
8. Allow the cake to cool in the pan for 15 minutes before transferring it to a wire rack to cool completely.
9. Dust the Vegan Chocolate Banana Kugelhopf with powdered

sugar before serving.

These gluten-free and vegan Kugelhopf options offer delicious alternatives for those with dietary restrictions or preferences. Enjoy the rich flavors of almond flour or the delightful combination of chocolate and banana in these special variations.

Chapter(8) Creative Decorations and Glazes for Kugelhopf:

a. Powdered Sugar Dusting:
Instructions:

1. Once the Kugelhopf is fully cooled, place a fine-mesh sieve over the cake.
2. Generously dust the top of the Kugelhopf with powdered sugar by tapping the sieve gently.
3. Ensure an even distribution for an elegant and classic finish.
4. Slice and serve the Kugelhopf, showcasing the beautiful powdered sugar dusting.

b. Drizzled Chocolate Ganache:
Ingredients for Chocolate Ganache:

- 1/2 cup dark chocolate chips
- 1/4 cup coconut cream or non-dairy milk

Instructions:

1. In a small saucepan, heat the coconut cream or non-dairy milk until it's just about to simmer.
2. Pour the hot liquid over the dark chocolate chips in a heatproof bowl. Let it sit for a minute.
3. Stir the mixture until smooth and glossy.
4. Allow the ganache to cool slightly.
5. Drizzle the chocolate ganache over the cooled Kugelhopf, letting it cascade down the sides.
6. Allow the ganache to set before slicing and serving the chocolate-drizzled Kugelhopf.

c. Citrus Glaze with Candied Zest:
Ingredients for Citrus Glaze:

- 1 cup powdered sugar
- 2-3 tablespoons fresh citrus juice (lemon, orange, or a combination)
- Zest of the citrus fruit for garnish

Instructions:

1. In a bowl, whisk together the powdered sugar and citrus juice until a smooth glaze forms.
2. Adjust the consistency by adding more sugar for thickness or more juice for a thinner glaze.
3. Once the Kugelhopf has cooled, drizzle the citrus glaze over the top.
4. Sprinkle the glazed Kugelhopf with finely grated candied citrus zest for a burst of flavor and visual appeal.
5. Allow the glaze to set before serving slices of the citrus-infused Kugelhopf.

These creative decorations and glazes add a finishing touch to your Kugelhopf, transforming it into a visually stunning and delectable treat. Choose the method that suits your taste, or experiment with a combination for a truly unique presentation. Enjoy the delightful textures and flavors these decorative elements bring to your Kugelhopf!

Chapter (9) Serving Suggestions for Kugelhopf:

a. Accompanying Sauces and Creams:
1.Vanilla Whipped Cream:

- Whip heavy cream or a non-dairy alternative until stiff peaks form. Add a touch of vanilla extract and a sprinkle of powdered sugar for sweetness. Serve a dollop alongside each slice of Kugelhopf.

2.Chocolate Sauce:

- Melt dark chocolate with a bit of coconut oil or non-dairy milk for a silky chocolate sauce. Drizzle it over individual slices or serve on the side for dipping.

3.Fruit Compote:

- Prepare a simple fruit compote by simmering fresh or frozen berries with a bit of sugar until they break down into a syrupy consistency. Spoon the compote over slices of Kugelhopf for a fruity burst.

4.Lemon Glaze:

- Combine powdered sugar with fresh lemon juice to create a tangy lemon glaze. Drizzle it over the Kugelhopf for a zesty contrast.

5.Almond Cream:

- Mix almond butter or almond extract with a bit of powdered sugar and non-dairy milk to create a smooth almond cream. Serve it as a decadent accompaniment.

b. Ideal Beverage Pairings:

Coffee:

The rich and varied flavors of Kugelhopf make it a perfect companion to a cup of freshly brewed coffee. Whether it's black coffee, a latte, or a cappuccino, the pairing enhances the overall experience.

Tea:

Pairing Kugelhopf with a cup of tea, such as Earl Grey or a fruity herbal blend, offers a delightful contrast. The aromatic tea complements the sweet or savory notes of the cake.

Hot Chocolate:

For a comforting and indulgent treat, serve Kugelhopf with a mug of hot chocolate. The combination of rich chocolate and the cake's texture creates a heavenly pairing.

Sparkling Wine or Champagne:

For special occasions, consider pairing Kugelhopf with a glass of sparkling wine or champagne. The effervescence cuts through the richness, creating a sophisticated and celebratory match.

Mulled Cider:

During the fall or winter months, a warm mug of mulled cider complements the seasonal flavors of pumpkin spice or cranberry-orange Kugelhopf.

Iced Tea or Lemonade:

In the summertime, a refreshing iced tea or lemonade pairs well with the fruity and citrus-infused variations of Kugelhopf.

Remember to consider personal preferences and the flavor profile of the specific Kugelhopf variation you've prepared when choosing accompanying sauces and beverages. These serving suggestions enhance the overall experience and make enjoying Kugelhopf a delightful culinary journey.

Chapter(10) Tips for Storing and Freezing Kugelhopf:

a. Proper Storage to Maintain Freshness:

Room Temperature Storage:

Keep Kugelhopf at room temperature for the first 1-2 days if it's going to be consumed within that time. Store it in an airtight container or wrap it tightly with plastic wrap.

Refrigeration:

If you need to store Kugelhopf for a longer period, especially if it contains perishable ingredients like fresh fruit or dairy, consider refrigerating it. Ensure it's well-wrapped to prevent it from drying out.

Avoid Direct Sunlight:

Store Kugelhopf in a cool, dark place away from direct sunlight. Exposure to sunlight can affect the texture and flavor of the cake.

Airtight Containers:

Use airtight containers or resealable plastic bags to preserve the freshness and prevent the cake from absorbing any unwanted odors.

Avoid the Fridge if Possible:

While refrigeration can extend the shelf life, it may impact the texture of the cake. If you can, store it at room temperature for the best taste and texture.

Slice and Freeze:

If you won't consume the entire Kugelhopf within a few days, consider slicing it before storing. This allows you to thaw only the slices you need, reducing waste.

b. Freezing Guidelines for Long-Term Enjoyment:
Wrap Properly:

If you plan to freeze the entire Kugelhopf, wrap it tightly in plastic wrap and then place it in a layer of aluminum foil or a resealable plastic bag to prevent freezer burn.

Individual Slices:

For convenience, slice the Kugelhopf into individual portions before freezing. Separate the slices with parchment paper to prevent sticking.

Double Protection:

If you're freezing slices, place them in a freezer-safe container with a tight-fitting lid. This adds an extra layer of protection against freezer odors.

Label and Date:

Clearly label the packaging with the date of freezing. This helps you keep track of how long the Kugelhopf has been in the freezer and ensures you can enjoy it at its best quality.

Thawing:

When ready to enjoy, thaw Kugelhopf in the refrigerator or at room temperature. Avoid using a microwave, as it can affect the texture.

Quality Check:

After thawing, check the texture and flavor. If the Kugelhopf has been properly stored, it should retain its delicious taste and moist texture.

By following these storage and freezing tips, you can prolong the freshness of your Kugelhopf and enjoy its delightful flavors over an extended period.

Chapter (11) International Kugelhopf Variations:

a. French-Inspired Champagne Kugelhopf:
Additional Ingredients:

- 1/2 cup champagne or sparkling wine
- Zest of 1 lemon

Instructions:

1. Incorporate champagne or sparkling wine into the batter during the mixing process for a touch of effervescence and flavor.
2. Add the zest of one lemon to enhance the citrus notes, complementing the champagne.
3. Follow the Mastering the Basic Kugelhopf Recipe steps, incorporating these French-inspired elements.
4. Dust the Champagne Kugelhopf with powdered sugar for an elegant finish.
5. Serve slices with a side of fresh berries for a delightful French-inspired treat.

b. Italian Amaretto and Espresso Kugelhopf:
Additional Ingredients:

- 1/4 cup amaretto liqueur
- 2 tablespoons finely ground espresso or coffee powder
- 1/2 cup chopped toasted almonds

Instructions:

1. Mix amaretto liqueur and finely ground espresso into the batter during the mixing process.
2. Fold in chopped toasted almonds for a delightful crunch and nutty flavor.
3. Follow the Mastering the Basic Kugelhopf Recipe steps, incorporating these Italian-inspired elements.
4. Drizzle the cooled Kugelhopf with a simple amaretto glaze made from powdered sugar and amaretto.
5. Serve slices with a side of whipped cream or a scoop of vanilla gelato for an indulgent Italian experience.

c. Scandinavian Cardamom and Cinnamon Kugelhopf:
Additional Ingredients:

- 1 teaspoon ground cardamom
- 1 teaspoon ground cinnamon
- 1/2 cup chopped walnuts or pecans

Instructions:

- Add ground cardamom and cinnamon to the batter during the mixing process for warm and aromatic Scandinavian flavors.
- Fold in chopped walnuts or pecans for added texture and nuttiness.
- Follow the Mastering the Basic Kugelhopf Recipe steps, incorporating these Scandinavian-inspired elements.
- Drizzle the cooled Kugelhopf with a simple glaze made from powdered sugar and a touch of cinnamon.
- Serve slices with a dollop of lightly sweetened whipped cream or a side of lingonberry jam for a Scandinavian twist.

These international Kugelhopf variations bring a taste of France, Italy, and Scandinavia to your table, showcasing the diversity and richness of flavors from around the world. Enjoy the global journey through these unique and delicious creations!

Chapter(12) Health-Conscious Kugelhopf Variations:

a. Whole Wheat and Honey Kugelhopf:
   Additional Ingredients:

- 2 cups whole wheat flour
- 1/2 cup honey
- 1/2 cup unsweetened applesauce
- 1/2 cup chopped nuts or seeds (e.g., walnuts or sunflower seeds)

Instructions:

1. Substitute whole wheat flour for part or all of the all-purpose flour to add fiber and nutrients.
2. Replace granulated sugar with honey for natural sweetness. Adjust the quantity based on your preferred level of sweetness.
3. Incorporate unsweetened applesauce into the batter to enhance moisture and reduce the need for additional fats.
4. Fold in chopped nuts or seeds for added crunch and a boost of healthy fats.
5. Follow the Mastering the Basic Kugelhopf Recipe steps, incorporating these health-conscious elements.
6. Dust the cooled Whole Wheat and Honey Kugelhopf with a touch of powdered sugar if desired.

b. Greek Yogurt and Berry Delight:
Additional Ingredients:

- 1 cup Greek yogurt
- 1 cup mixed berries (e.g., blueberries, raspberries, strawberries)

Instructions:

1. Replace a portion of the milk with Greek yogurt to increase protein and create a moist crumb.
2. Gently fold mixed berries into the batter before pouring it into the pan for a burst of natural sweetness and antioxidants.
3. Follow the Mastering the Basic Kugelhopf Recipe steps, incorporating these health-conscious elements.
4. Serve slices with an additional dollop of Greek yogurt and a handful of fresh berries for a delightful and nutritious treat.

c. Nut-Free Banana Oat Kugelhopf:
Additional Ingredients:

- 1 cup rolled oats
- 1/2 cup mashed ripe bananas
- 1/2 cup dairy-free milk (e.g., almond milk or oat milk)
- 1/2 cup dried fruit (e.g., raisins or chopped dates)

Instructions:

1. Replace a portion of the flour with rolled oats for added fiber and a hearty texture.
2. Mash ripe bananas and fold them into the batter for natural sweetness and moisture.
3. Substitute dairy-free milk for regular milk for a lactose-free option.
4. Add dried fruit for bursts of sweetness without the use of nuts.
5. Follow the Mastering the Basic Kugelhopf Recipe steps, incorporating these health-conscious elements.
6. Drizzle the cooled Banana Oat Kugelhopf with a simple glaze made from powdered sugar and a touch of banana puree.

These health-conscious Kugelhopf variations prioritize whole grains, natural sweeteners, and nutrient-rich ingredients, offering a guilt-free indulgence for those seeking a balance between flavor and wellness. Enjoy these wholesome and delicious options!

Chapter (13) Kugelhopf Baking for Special Occasions:

a. Elegant Wedding Cake Kugelhopf:
Additional Ingredients and Decorations:

- White chocolate ganache for drizzling
- Edible flowers or fondant flowers for decoration
- Silver or gold edible dust for a touch of elegance

Instructions:

1. Follow the Mastering the Basic Kugelhopf Recipe, ensuring a flawless texture and flavor.
2. Instead of powdered sugar, drizzle the cooled Kugelhopf with white chocolate ganache for a luxurious finish.
3. Decorate the Kugelhopf with edible flowers or fondant flowers, creating a beautiful and elegant design.
4. Lightly dust the flowers or the entire Kugelhopf with silver or gold edible dust for a touch of glamour.
5. Present the Elegant Wedding Cake Kugelhopf as a stunning centerpiece for weddings, bridal showers, or any special celebration.

b. Festive Holiday Wreath Kugelhopf:
Additional Ingredients and Decorations:

- Red and green marzipan or fondant for shaping into holly leaves and berries
- Powdered sugar for dusting
- Rosemary sprigs for a natural wreath appearance

Instructions:

1. Create a wreath shape using marzipan or fondant leaves and berries, placing it on top of the Kugelhopf before baking.
2. Follow the Mastering the Basic Kugelhopf Recipe, ensuring the wreath maintains its shape during baking.
3. Dust the entire Kugelhopf with powdered sugar for a snowy effect.
4. Garnish with additional marzipan or fondant leaves and berries for a festive touch.
5. Add rosemary sprigs around the base of the Kugelhopf for a natural and aromatic holiday wreath.
6. Present the Festive Holiday Wreath Kugelhopf as a delightful centerpiece for Christmas or other winter celebrations.

c. Birthday Celebration Kugelhopf Tower:
Additional Ingredients and Decorations:

- Vibrant-colored icing for drizzling or piping
- Colorful sprinkles or edible glitter for a celebratory touch
- Small birthday candles or decorative cake toppers

Instructions:

1. Drizzle or pipe vibrant-colored icing over the cooled Kugelhopf in a decorative pattern.
2. Sprinkle colorful sprinkles or edible glitter over the icing for a festive and celebratory appearance.
3. Add small birthday candles or decorative cake toppers to the top of the Kugelhopf for extra flair.
4. Stack multiple Kugelhopfs of varying sizes to create a tower effect, securing each layer with a small amount of icing.
5. Present the Birthday Celebration Kugelhopf Tower as a unique and delicious alternative to a traditional birthday cake.

These special occasion Kugelhopf variations are designed to impress and delight, adding a touch of sophistication and celebration to weddings, holidays, and birthdays. Enjoy the joy and flavor of these festive creations!

Chapter (14) DIY Kugelhopf Gifts:

a. Personalized Kugelhopf Mix Jars:
Materials:

- Clear glass jars
- Decorative labels, ribbons, and gift tags
- Ingredients for the Kugelhopf mix (flour, sugar, baking powder, etc.)
- Small recipe card or note

Instructions:

1. Layer the Ingredients: Begin by carefully layering the dry ingredients for the Kugelhopf in the glass jars. Create visually appealing layers for an added touch.
2. Decorate the Jars: Once the jars are filled, attach decorative labels and tie colorful ribbons around the necks. This adds a personal and festive flair.
3. Attach Baking Instructions: Include a thoughtful gift tag with baking instructions, specifying any additional wet ingredients required for completing the Kugelhopf.
4. Personalized Note: Enhance the personal touch by adding a small recipe card or note with a personal message, sharing your love for baking.
5. Present with Love: These personalized Kugelhopf mix jars make delightful gifts for friends and family who can enjoy the experience of baking their own delicious treat. It's a thoughtful and creative way to share the joy of homemade goodies.

b. Kugelhopf Gift Baskets:
Materials:

- Wicker baskets or decorative boxes
- Tissue paper or shredded paper
- Individual Kugelhopf slices or mini Kugelhopfs
- Assorted sauces, jams, or spreads
- Tea or coffee selection
- Small note or card with a personalized message

Instructions:

1. Arrange the Basket: Line the basket with colorful tissue paper or shredded paper, creating a visually appealing and cushioned base.
2. Add Kugelhopf Treats: Arrange individual slices or mini Kugelhopfs in the basket, ensuring an attractive presentation.
3. Include Accompaniments: Enhance the gift basket with jars of sauces, jams, or spreads that pair perfectly with Kugelhopf. Consider adding a selection of high-quality tea or coffee for a complete and indulgent experience.
4. Write a Heartfelt Note: Include a small note or card expressing your well wishes or a personalized message, conveying the warmth of your intentions.
5. Wrap and Present: Wrap the entire basket with cellophane or a decorative wrap, securing it with a beautiful ribbon. Present this delightful Kugelhopf gift basket for birthdays, holidays, or special occasions. It's a comprehensive treat that caters to a variety of tastes.

c. Kugelhopf Mug Cake Kits:
Materials:

- Decorative mugs
- Ingredients for individual Kugelhopf mug cakes

- Mini chocolate chips, dried fruit, or nuts (optional)
- Gift tags with mug cake instructions

Instructions:

1. Layer the Ingredients: In each mug, layer the dry ingredients for the Kugelhopf mug cake. Add optional ingredients like mini chocolate chips, dried fruit, or nuts for extra flavor and texture.
2. Attach Instructions: Attach a charming gift tag with clear instructions for preparing the mug cake. Specify any necessary wet ingredients and microwave times.
3. Decorate the Mugs: Decorate the mugs with festive ribbons or personalized touches, making them visually appealing and ready for gifting.
4. Arrange in a Gift Box: Place the mugs in a decorative gift box, ensuring they are securely nestled to prevent breakage during transportation.
5. Gift with Warmth: Share these Kugelhopf Mug Cake Kits with friends or colleagues for a delightful and convenient way to enjoy a warm and freshly baked treat in the comfort of their own mug. It's a thoughtful gesture that brings the joy of homemade goodies to their homes.

These extended DIY Kugelhopf gift ideas allow you to share the delight of this delicious treat with your loved ones in a thoughtful, creative, and personalized way.

Whether it's a beautifully layered mix jar, a comprehensive gift basket, or a convenient mug cake kit, these gifts are sure to bring smiles and appreciation.

Chapter (15) Retro-Inspired Kugelhopf Variations:

a. Pineapple Upside-Down Kugelhopf:
Additional Ingredients:

- Pineapple slices (canned or fresh)
- Maraschino cherries
- Brown sugar

Instructions:

1. Grease the Kugelhopf pan and line the bottom with pineapple slices.
2. Place a maraschino cherry in the center of each pineapple slice.
3. Sprinkle brown sugar over the pineapples, creating a caramelized layer.
4. Prepare the Kugelhopf batter following the Mastering the Basic Kugelhopf Recipe.
5. Carefully pour the batter over the pineapple layer in the pan.
6. Bake as directed, ensuring the Kugelhopf is thoroughly cooked.
7. Once cooled, invert the pan to reveal the retro-inspired Pineapple Upside-Down Kugelhopf.

b. Rum Raisin and Walnut Kugelhopf:
Additional Ingredients:

- 1/2 cup dark rum
- 1/2 cup raisins
- 1/2 cup chopped walnuts

Instructions:

1. In a bowl, soak raisins in dark rum for at least an hour or until plump.
2. Drain the excess rum from the raisins and reserve it for later.
3. Fold the plumped raisins and chopped walnuts into the Kugelhopf batter during the mixing process.
4. Bake the Rum Raisin and Walnut Kugelhopf as per the Mastering the Basic Kugelhopf Recipe.
5. While the Kugelhopf is still warm, brush the top with the reserved rum for an extra layer of flavor.
6. Allow the Kugelhopf to cool completely before serving.

c. Orange Creamsicle Kugelhopf:
Additional Ingredients:

- Zest of 2 oranges
- 1/2 cup orange juice
- 1/2 cup vanilla yogurt
- Orange glaze (powdered sugar and orange juice)

Instructions:

1. Add the zest of two oranges to the Kugelhopf batter during the mixing process for a citrusy aroma.
2. Substitute a portion of the milk with freshly squeezed orange juice to infuse the batter with a zesty flavor.
3. Fold vanilla yogurt into the batter for a creamy and tangy element.
4. Follow the Mastering the Basic Kugelhopf Recipe steps, incorporating these retro-inspired elements.
5. Prepare an orange glaze using powdered sugar and a small amount of orange juice. Drizzle it over the cooled Orange Creamsicle Kugelhopf for a sweet and citrusy finish.

These retro-inspired Kugelhopf variations take cues from classic flavors and desserts, adding a nostalgic twist to this beloved treat. Enjoy the unique and delightful taste of Pineapple Upside-Down, Rum Raisin and Walnut, and Orange Creamsicle Kugelhopf!

Chapter (16) Exotic Flavor Adventures:

a. Cardamom Rose Pistachio Kugelhopf:
Additional Ingredients:

- 1 teaspoon ground cardamom
- 1 tablespoon rose water
- 1/2 cup crushed pistachios

Instructions:

1. Add ground cardamom and rose water to the Kugelhopf batter during the mixing process for a fragrant and exotic twist.
2. Fold crushed pistachios into the batter to infuse the Kugelhopf with a delightful crunch and nutty flavor.
3. Follow the Mastering the Basic Kugelhopf Recipe steps, incorporating these exotic elements.
4. Once cooled, sprinkle the top with additional crushed pistachios for a visually appealing finish.

b. Mango Coconut Bliss Kugelhopf:
Additional Ingredients:

- 1/2 cup mango puree
- 1/2 cup shredded coconut
- Zest of 1 lime

Instructions:

1. Incorporate mango puree into the Kugelhopf batter during the mixing process for a tropical and fruity flavor.
2. Fold shredded coconut into the batter to add a sweet and chewy texture reminiscent of the tropics.
3. Add the zest of one lime for a hint of citrus brightness.
4. Follow the Mastering the Basic Kugelhopf Recipe steps, incorporating these exotic elements.
5. Once cooled, drizzle the Kugelhopf with a lime glaze made from powdered sugar and lime juice for an extra burst of flavor.

**c. Matcha Green Tea and White Chocolate Kugelhopf:
Additional Ingredients:**

- 1 tablespoon matcha green tea powder
- 1/2 cup white chocolate chips
- Matcha glaze (powdered sugar and matcha green tea powder)

Instructions:

1. Add matcha green tea powder to the Kugelhopf batter during the mixing process for a vibrant green color and earthy flavor.
2. Fold white chocolate chips into the batter to create pockets of creamy sweetness.
3. Follow the Mastering the Basic Kugelhopf Recipe steps, incorporating these exotic elements.
4. Once cooled, drizzle the Kugelhopf with a matcha glaze made from powdered sugar and matcha green tea powder for a visually stunning and delicious finish.

These exotic flavor adventures bring a world of tastes to your Kugelhopf, showcasing the unique and delightful combinations of Cardamom Rose Pistachio, Mango Coconut Bliss, and Matcha Green Tea and White Chocolate. Enjoy the journey of flavors with these exotic twists on a classic favorite!

Chapter (17)Kugelhopf for Breakfast:

a. Maple Pecan Breakfast Kugelhopf:
Additional Ingredients:

- 1/2 cup pure maple syrup
- 1/2 cup chopped pecans
- 1 teaspoon ground cinnamon
- Powdered sugar for dusting

Instructions:

1. Start your day with the comforting aroma of the Maple Pecan Breakfast Kugelhopf by adding pure maple syrup and ground cinnamon to the batter during the mixing process. These ingredients infuse the cake with a warm sweetness that evokes cozy mornings.
2. Fold in chopped pecans to provide a delightful crunch and a nutty richness, creating a texture that complements the soft crumb of the Kugelhopf.
3. Follow the Mastering the Basic Kugelhopf Recipe steps, ensuring that the batter is well-mixed and baked to perfection.
4. After cooling, generously drizzle the top with additional maple syrup, creating a luscious glaze that enhances the sweetness. Finish it off with a dusting of powdered sugar for an extra touch of elegance.
5. Serve slices of this Maple Pecan Breakfast Kugelhopf alongside your favorite hot beverage for a comforting and indulgent morning treat.

b. Apple Cinnamon Streusel Morning Kugelhopf:
Additional Ingredients:

- 1 cup finely chopped apples (peeled and cored)
- 1 teaspoon ground cinnamon
- Streusel topping (1/2 cup flour, 1/4 cup brown sugar, 1/4 cup cold butter, diced)

Instructions:

1. Wake up your taste buds with the Apple Cinnamon Streusel Morning Kugelhopf by incorporating finely chopped apples and ground cinnamon into the batter during the mixing process. These ingredients create a delightful fruity and aromatic flavor.

2. Prepare a streusel topping by combining flour, brown sugar, and cold diced butter. Sprinkle this crumbly mixture generously over the batter before baking, adding a layer of sweetness and texture to the Kugelhopf.

3. Follow the Mastering the Basic Kugelhopf Recipe steps, ensuring the streusel-topped batter bakes into a moist and flavorful breakfast delight.

4. Once cooled, slice the Apple Cinnamon Streusel Morning Kugelhopf and savor each bite, enjoying the combination of soft apple pieces, warm cinnamon, and the satisfying crunch of the streusel topping.

5. Pair this breakfast treat with a cup of freshly brewed coffee or hot tea to kickstart your day on a delicious note.

c. Savory Bacon and Cheddar Breakfast Kugelhopf:
   Additional Ingredients:

- 1/2 cup cooked and crumbled bacon
- 1/2 cup shredded cheddar cheese
- 1 tablespoon chopped chives

- Sour cream or cream cheese for serving

Instructions:

1. Add a savory twist to your morning routine with the Savory Bacon and Cheddar Breakfast Kugelhopf. Fold cooked and crumbled bacon, shredded cheddar cheese, and chopped chives into the batter during the mixing process for a delightful combination of flavors.
2. Follow the Mastering the Basic Kugelhopf Recipe steps, ensuring that the savory elements are evenly distributed throughout the batter.
3. Once baked, allow the Kugelhopf to cool slightly before slicing. The aroma of smoky bacon and melted cheddar will make your kitchen feel like a gourmet breakfast haven.
4. Serve slices with a dollop of sour cream or cream cheese for a creamy and tangy contrast that elevates the savory experience.
5. Enjoy this savory breakfast creation alongside a refreshing glass of juice or a cup of herbal tea, making your morning memorable and satisfying.

These breakfast-inspired Kugelhopf variations offer a range of flavors, from the sweet warmth of Maple Pecan to the comforting aroma of Apple Cinnamon Streusel, and the savory goodness of Bacon and Cheddar.

They are perfect for turning an ordinary morning into a delightful culinary experience. Start your day on a delicious note with these unique and flavorful breakfast treats!

Chapter (18) Kugelhopf Artistry: Advanced Techniques

a. Marbling and Swirling Techniques:
   Additional Ingredients:

- Multiple colors of food coloring or natural dyes
- Flavored extracts (e.g., vanilla, almond, citrus)

Instructions:

1. Divide the Kugelhopf batter into separate bowls.
2. Add different colors of food coloring or natural dyes to each bowl, creating a vibrant palette.
3. Incorporate flavored extracts into each colored batter for added depth of flavor.
4. Spoon the colored batters into the Kugelhopf pan in a random pattern.
5. Use a skewer or knife to swirl and marble the colors together, creating a visually stunning effect.
6. Follow the Mastering the Basic Kugelhopf Recipe steps, ensuring that the marbling and swirling techniques are maintained during the baking process.
7. Once cooled, marvel at your Marbling and Swirling Techniques Kugelhopf, a true work of edible art.

b. Multi-Layered Kugelhopf Creations:
Additional Ingredients:

- Separate batches of flavored and colored batters
- Fillings such as chocolate chips, dried fruit, or nuts

Instructions:

1. Prepare multiple batches of Kugelhopf batter, each with a unique flavor and color.
2. Layer the different batters in the Kugelhopf pan, creating distinct and colorful strata.
3. Intersperse each layer with fillings like chocolate chips, dried fruit, or nuts for added texture and flavor.
4. Follow the Mastering the Basic Kugelhopf Recipe steps, ensuring that the layers are maintained during baking.
5. Once cooled, slice into the Multi-Layered Kugelhopf to reveal a spectacular display of colors and flavors.
6. This visually stunning and flavorful creation is sure to impress both the eyes and the taste buds.

c. Sculpted Kugelhopf Masterpieces:
Additional Tools:

- Specialty cake molds or silicone molds
- Pastry brushes for intricate detailing
- Edible gold or silver leaf (optional)

Instructions:

1. Obtain a specialty cake or silicone mold that imparts a unique shape to the Kugelhopf.
2. Prepare the Kugelhopf batter and carefully pour it into the intricately shaped mold.
3. Use pastry brushes to ensure the batter reaches all the nooks and crannies of the mold for a detailed and defined result.
4. Follow the Mastering the Basic Kugelhopf Recipe steps, adjusting the baking time if necessary to accommodate the specialized mold.
5. Once baked and cooled, consider adding an extra touch of luxury by applying edible gold or silver leaf to certain details of your Sculpted Kugelhopf Masterpiece.
6. Display your sculpted creation as a centerpiece, celebrating the fusion of culinary artistry and delightful flavors.

These advanced Kugelhopf artistry techniques allow you to elevate this classic treat into a visual masterpiece. Whether you opt for the captivating Marbling and Swirling Techniques, the multi-layered wonder of Multi-Layered Kugelhopf Creations, or the intricate beauty of Sculpted Kugelhopf Masterpieces, each creation is a testament to your culinary creativity and skill. Enjoy the process of crafting these edible works of art!

Chapter (19) Kugelhopf Pairings with Accompaniments:

a. Homemade Whipped Creams and Frostings:
Whipped Cream Variations:

- Classic Vanilla Whipped Cream
- Chocolate Espresso Whipped Cream
- Citrus Zest Infused Whipped Cream

Frosting Options:

- Cream Cheese Frosting with a Hint of Lemon
- White Chocolate Ganache Drizzle
- Maple Buttercream Frosting

Instructions:

1. Prepare your favorite homemade whipped cream or frosting variation.
2. Serve a slice of your chosen Kugelhopf with a dollop or drizzle of the whipped cream or frosting.
3. Garnish with complementary ingredients like chocolate shavings, citrus zest, or chopped nuts.
4. Experiment with different pairings to find your perfect flavor combination.
5. The velvety textures of whipped creams and the richness of frostings enhance the experience of your Kugelhopf, turning it into a luxurious treat.

b. Ice Cream Complements:
Ice Cream Flavors:

- Vanilla Bean
- Salted Caramel Swirl
- Dark Chocolate
- Butter Pecan

Serving Suggestions:

1. Place a generous scoop of your favorite ice cream alongside a warm slice of Kugelhopf.
2. Allow the ice cream to slightly melt, creating a decadent sauce that envelops the Kugelhopf.
3. Top with additional treats such as caramel sauce, hot fudge, or crushed nuts for added indulgence.
4. The combination of warm Kugelhopf and cold, creamy ice cream offers a delightful contrast of temperatures and textures.

c. Fresh Fruit Salsas and Compotes:
Fruit Salsa Options:

- Strawberry Mint Salsa
- Pineapple Mango Jalapeño Salsa
- Mixed Berry Basil Salsa

Compote Variations:

- Orange Cardamom Compote
- Cinnamon Apple Compote
- Balsamic Berry Compote

Instructions:

1. Prepare a vibrant fruit salsa or a flavorful compote.
2. Spoon the fruit salsa over slices of Kugelhopf, adding a burst of freshness and a hint of spice.
3. Alternatively, drizzle warm compote over the Kugelhopf, allowing the flavors to meld.
4. Serve with a dollop of whipped cream or a scoop of vanilla ice cream for an extra layer of deliciousness.
5. The combination of the sweet, moist Kugelhopf with the bright and tangy fruit elements creates a symphony of flavors that's perfect for dessert or a special breakfast.

These Kugelhopf accompaniments offer a myriad of flavors and textures that can be tailored to suit your taste preferences.

Whether you're indulging in the luxurious notes of homemade whipped creams and frostings, enjoying the contrast of warm Kugelhopf with cold ice cream, or savoring the bright, fruity elements of fresh fruit salsas and compotes, each pairing promises a delightful culinary experience.

❖ Conclusion:

In the delightful journey through "Kugelhopf Delights: A Culinary Journey Through Irresistible Bundt Cakes," we've explored a multitude of flavors, techniques, and creative possibilities. As we wrap up this culinary adventure, let's take a moment to recap the key techniques, encourage further experimentation, and extend an invitation to share your Kugelhopf creations and experiences.

Recap of Key Techniques:

- Mastering the Basics: Understand the foundational steps of crafting a perfect Kugelhopf, from choosing the right pan to achieving the ideal texture and flavor.
- Flavor Variations: Explore a diverse range of flavors, from classic almond to exotic combinations like Cardamom Rose Pistachio and Matcha Green Tea with White Chocolate.
- Artistic Creations: Elevate your Kugelhopf into a visual masterpiece through marbling, swirling, multi-layering, or sculpting techniques.

Encouragement for Experimentation:

The beauty of Kugelhopf lies in its versatility. Feel free to experiment with unique ingredients, create your own flavor combinations, and explore various artistic presentations. Whether you're a seasoned baker or just starting, the kitchen is your canvas, and Kugelhopf is your medium for culinary expression.

Invitation to Share Kugelhopf Creations and Experiences:

We invite you to share your Kugelhopf creations and experiences with the global community of baking enthusiasts. Whether it's a personal twist on a classic recipe or a completely innovative creation, your journey in the kitchen is worth celebrating. Share your insights, photos, and stories on social media platforms, baking forums, or with friends and family.

As you continue your exploration of the culinary arts, remember that each Kugelhopf is a unique expression of your creativity and passion for baking. Whether enjoyed as a comforting breakfast, a decadent dessert, or a show-stopping centerpiece, your Kugelhopf creations are sure to bring joy and satisfaction to those fortunate enough to experience them.

Happy baking, and may your Kugelhopf adventures be as delightful as the flavors they carry!

www.ingramcontent.com/pod-product-compliance
Lightning Source LLC
Chambersburg PA
CBHW021320160726
47994CB00004B/1537